GEO

ALLEN COUNTY PUBLIC LIBRARY

3 1833 03289 7222

P9-ECX-820

j937                                        7/98
McNeill, Sarah.
Ancient Romans at a glance

## ALLEN COUNTY PUBLIC LIBRARY
## FORT WAYNE, INDIANA 46802

You may return this book to any agency, branch,
or bookmobile of the Allen County Public Library

DEMCO

# ANCIENT ROMANS

## AT A GLANCE

DR SARAH MCNEILL

PETER BEDRICK BOOKS

NEW YORK

Allen County Public Library
900 Webster Street
PO Box 2270
Fort Wayne, IN 46801-2270

Published by
PETER BEDRICK BOOKS
156 Fifth Avenue
New York, NY 10010

© Macdonald Young Books 1998

Designed by: The Design Works, Reading
Edited by: Lisa Edwards
Illustrated by: Maltings Partnership

All rights reserved. No part of this book may be reproduced, stored in
a retrieval system or transmitted by any other means, electronic,
mechanical, photocopying or otherwise, without the prior permission
of the publisher.

Library of Congress Cataloging-in-Publication Data available

First edition, 1997
Printed in Hong Kong

# CONTENTS

## TIME TRACK 6

What happened when in Ancient Rome, the Roman Empire and around the world

## SITE-SEEING – A GUIDE TO THE ROMAN WORLD 8

Where to find the most important places

## EMPIRE-BUILDING 10

Where the Roman Empire began and how it grew; how people traded and traveled around the Empire; how people paid for things

## ROMAN SOCIETY 12

How the Republic was formed; who Roman officials were; what Roman citizenship entitled people to; what jobs people did; how slaves lived; what Roman law was

## EMINENT EMPERORS 14

How the Republic ended; who the first Roman emperor was; how the most famous emperors lived and ruled; timeline

## ROMAN LIFE 16

Where people lived; what life in a town was like; what food people ate and how they dined; how people dressed; what family life was like

## ROMANS AT PLAY 18

What games and sports the Romans enjoyed; where they were played; how Romans danced and played music; what Roman theater was; how people used public baths

## GODS AND GODDESSES 20

Which gods the Romans worshiped; where they worshiped; what happened on festival days; how the Romans tried to communicate with their gods

## ROMANS AT WAR 22

How the Roman army was organized; how soldiers were trained; what equipment and weapons were used; how battles were fought and towns captured; how soldiers built forts

## BUILDINGS, ENGINEERING AND INVENTIONS 24

How the Romans built roads, bridges and buildings; which were the biggest Roman buildings; how they invented heating systems; timeline

## WORDS AND PICTURES 26

What language the Romans used; why public speaking was an important skill; how the modern calendar was formed; how Roman artists worked; who the most famous Roman writers and speakers were; timeline

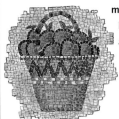

## THE END OF THE EMPIRE 28

Who Rome's enemies were; how the Empire fell; how Christianity spread throughout the Empire; what the Byzantine Empire was; timeline

## GLOSSARY AND INDEX 30

# TIME TRACK

## ROME AND THE ANCIENT WORLD

From about 500 BC, the people of Rome built the first great Empire of the western world. Emperors ruled in Rome until AD 476. Throughout the Empire, the Romans promoted trade, learning, peace and the rule of law. They spread civilized life by taking ideas and customs from one land to use in another. This spread of ideas lasted even when the Romans lost political power. It was the Romans' greatest achievement.

▼

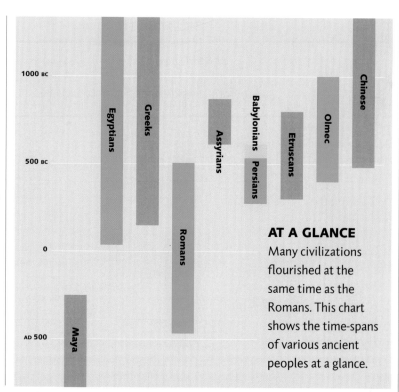

### AT A GLANCE

Many civilizations flourished at the same time as the Romans. This chart shows the time-spans of various ancient peoples at a glance.

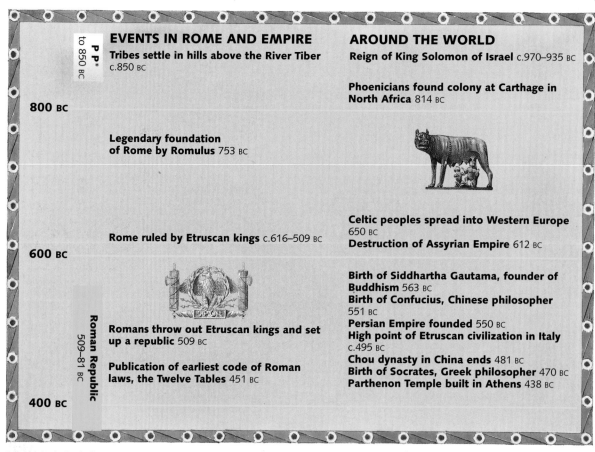

| EVENTS IN ROME AND EMPIRE | AROUND THE WORLD |
|---|---|
| **P P*** to 850 BC — **Tribes settle in hills above the River Tiber** c.850 BC | **Reign of King Solomon of Israel** c.970–935 BC |
| **800 BC** | **Phoenicians found colony at Carthage in North Africa** 814 BC |
| **Legendary foundation of Rome by Romulus** 753 BC | |
| | **Celtic peoples spread into Western Europe** 650 BC |
| **Rome ruled by Etruscan kings** c.616–509 BC | **Destruction of Assyrian Empire** 612 BC |
| **600 BC** | **Birth of Siddhartha Gautama, founder of Buddhism** 563 BC |
| | **Birth of Confucius, Chinese philosopher** 551 BC |
| | **Persian Empire founded** 550 BC |
| **Roman Republic 509–81 BC** — **Romans throw out Etruscan kings and set up a republic** 509 BC | **High point of Etruscan civilization in Italy** c.495 BC |
| | **Chou dynasty in China ends** 481 BC |
| **Publication of earliest code of Roman laws, the Twelve Tables** 451 BC | **Birth of Socrates, Greek philosopher** 470 BC |
| | **Parthenon Temple built in Athens** 438 BC |
| **400 BC** | |

## EVENTS IN ROME AND EMPIRE

| | |
|---|---|
| **400 BC** | |

**Roman Republic 509–81 BC**

Rome's first highway (Via Appia) and aqueduct built 312 BC
Rome controls all central and southern Italy 275 BC
Earliest record of gladiator fight 264 BC
Wars with Carthaginians 264–241 BC 218–201 BC
First Roman provinces set up in Sicily, Sardinia and Corsica 241 BC
Hannibal crosses the Alps and invades Italy, but fails to take Rome 218–7 BC

**200 BC**

Rome destroys Carthage and sets up province in Africa 146 BC
Rome conquers Greece and sets up province of Macedonia 146 BC
Unsuccessful slave revolt led by Spartacus 73–71 BC
Julius Caesar conquers Gaul 58–50 BC
First public library founded 39 BC
Augustus becomes first Roman emperor 27 BC

RD† T‡

**0**

**Emperors rule from Rome 27 BC–AD 395**

Start of the conquest of Britain AD 43
Fire destroys much of Rome AD 64
Persecution of Christians begins C.AD 64
Colosseum built in Rome AD 79
Eruption of Vesuvius destroys cities of Pompeii and Herculaneum AD 79
The Empire is at its greatest AD 117
Hadrian's Wall is built across Britain AD 125

**AD 200**

Parts of the Empire are invaded by Goths and other enemies AD 252
Constantine allows Christians to worship freely AD 313
Constantine creates Constantinople, a new capital city in the east AD 330

The Empire is divided; one center in Rome and the other in Constantinople AD 395

**AD 400**

**Emperors rule E. Empire from Constantinople AD 395 onward**

Rome is sacked by the Goths AD 410
Attila and his Huns invade Italy AD 452
Vandals sack Rome AD 455
The last emperor in the west is overthrown AD 476

The Eastern Empire (the Byzantine Empire) continues until AD 1453, when the Turks seize Constantinople

**AD 600**

## AROUND THE WORLD

Birth of Aristotle, Greek philosopher 384 BC
Alexander the Great invades India 326–5 BC
Mauryan dynasty founded in India 319 BC
Ptolemy builds library at Alexandria 290 BC

Qin Dynasty unites China; Great Wall of China built 221 BC
Mayan civilization develops in Central America c.200 BC

Death of Jesus Christ C.AD 33
Paper invented in China C.AD 105

End of Han dynasty in China AD 220

Moche culture begins in Peru C.AD 300

Chandragupta crowned emperor of northern India AD 320

Japan ruled by its first emperors AD 400

Mayan civilization flourishes AD 470

Mohammed, Prophet of Islam, born in Mecca AD 570

# SITE-SEEING – A GUIDE TO THE ANCIENT ROMAN WORLD

This map shows some of the most famous sites in the Roman Empire. The Romans built one of the greatest empires of all time; at its height it covered much of the western world. Forty-three Roman provinces stretched from North Africa in the south, to Britain and Germany in the north, and parts of Asia in the east. Some of these provinces were ruled by the Romans for 1,000 years.

HADRIAN'S WALL

BRITAIN

R. RHINE

Trier
GERMANY

FRANCE
(GAUL)

Nîmes

Ravenna

RIVER DANUBE

Segovia

SPAIN

Rome ITALY
Ostia
Pompeii and
Herculaneum

Constantinople

ASIA

GREECE

Athens

Carthage

MEDITERRANEAN SEA

NORTH AFRICA

Alexandria

EGYPT

RIVER NILE

**Hadrian's Wall**, begun in AD 122, was built to protect the Roman province of Britain from attacks by tribes from the north.

**Trier**, in Germany, became an important center of power when the emperor's court was set up there in about AD 200.

**Nîmes** was the one of several cities that the Romans built in southern Gaul (France). Many monuments survive here, including a temple, an amphitheater and an aqueduct.

 At **Segovia** in Spain, Roman engineers built a great aqueduct with 128 arches, to bring water to the city.

## THE ANCIENT CITY OF ROME

Rome was the center of the Roman world. You can still see many of its ancient buildings today. There were law courts, government buildings and temples situated in the Forum – the heart of the city.

**KEY**

1 **Palatine Hill** – site of the Emperor's Palace and home to wealthy Romans

2 **Baths of Caracalla** – public baths

3 **Colosseum** – sports arena

4 **Forum** – city center

5 **Circus Maximus** – racing arena

6 **River Tiber**

7 **City walls** – as they were after AD 275

PARTHIA

BLACK SEA

RIVER EUPHRATES

• Jerusalem

RED SEA

 **Rome** was built on seven hills above the River Tiber. According to legend two boys, Romulus and Remus, were brought up by a she-wolf on the Palatine Hill. It was Romulus who founded the city.

**Ostia**, a trading port on the River Tiber, supplied the city of Rome with goods from all over the Empire.

**Ravenna** became the emperor's capital city in the west in AD 402, when barbarian tribes from the east were attacking Rome.

 The towns of **Pompeii** and **Herculaneum** were buried in mud and ashes when the volcano Vesuvius erupted in AD 79. Volcanic ash preserved the towns so that we are able to see how the people of these cities lived.

**Alexandria** was the chief city in Egypt when the Romans took power there in 30 BC. Egypt was very important to the Romans because of its wealth and the crops grown there.

 **Constantinople** was built in AD 330. This Greek city in the east was rebuilt for Emperor Constantine, as a new Christian capital.

**Parthia**, a powerful kingdom in Asia, was one of Rome's most difficult enemies. Rome gave up the attempt to keep the land it held there.

 **Athens** was the center of the Greek civilization and under Roman rule it remained a great center of learning. The Romans adopted many Greek ideas, especially in law, science and art.

 **Carthage**, founded by the Phoenicians, was a powerful trading city. Rome fought three wars (the Punic Wars) with Carthage, destroying its position as a Mediterranean power and finally the city itself.

**Jerusalem** was the capital of the ancient Jewish state. Jesus Christ, the founder of Christianity, was crucified by the Romans in this city.

# EMPIRE-BUILDING

The first Romans were shepherds. They settled on the seven hills above the River Tiber in about 850 BC. At this time Italy was home to many different tribes and the people of Rome were just one of these tribes – called Latins. By about the sixth century BC Rome became a town, then a magnificent city. The Romans became very powerful in other lands. They conquered tribes in Italy, then those around the Mediterranean, and finally people in lands further away still, such as in Britain and Germany.

## IMPERIAL POST

The Emperor Augustus set up an Imperial postal service, to get messages to the countries of his Empire. At first, he used relays of runners. Later, horse carts were used and they could travel up to 45 miles in a day.

## TRADING PLACES

Trade flourished in the Empire. Merchants followed the Roman armies, growing rich by providing food and other goods for the soldiers. As Rome conquered far-off lands, this encouraged long distance trade. Goods from all over the Empire made their way to wealthy customers in Rome.

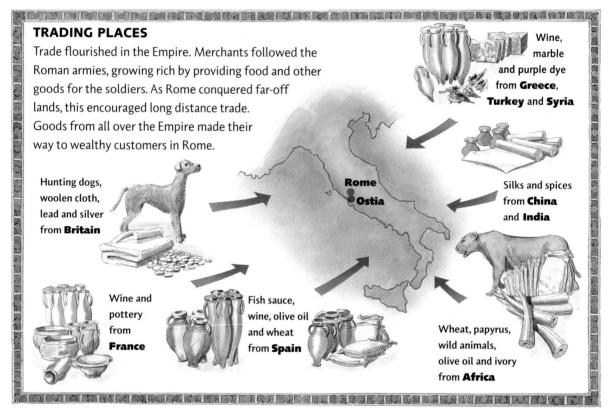

Wine, marble and purple dye from **Greece**, **Turkey** and **Syria**

Hunting dogs, woolen cloth, lead and silver from **Britain**

**Rome**
**Ostia**

Silks and spices from **China** and **India**

Wine and pottery from **France**

Fish sauce, wine, olive oil and wheat from **Spain**

Wheat, papyrus, wild animals, olive oil and ivory from **Africa**

**1** The extent of the Roman Empire in **100 BC**

**2** The extent of the Roman Empire in **44 BC**

Copper, silver and gold coins were used for trade and paying taxes in Rome and throughout the Empire. Often, during the time of Empire, they were stamped with the emperor's head. Sometimes, the emperor's military conquests or building projects appeared on the back.

## WEIGHT-WATCHERS

Roman traders had two devices for weighing goods – scales or a steelyard. Officials frequently checked weights to stop traders from cheating.

**A steelyard**

The weight was moved along the arm until it balanced with the goods.

The item being weighed was held by a hook.

### THE SPREAD OF EMPIRE

These maps show how the Roman Empire developed over a period of just 200 years. By AD 117 it reached its height, stretching all the way from Britain to Egypt, and from Spain across to the Middle East. ▼

## TRAVEL BY LAND AND SEA

The Romans needed to reach the furthest parts of their territories easily if they were to stay in control of their empire. So a great network of roads was built (see page 24). These routes were used by Roman officials, the army and by traders. ▼

Goods were carried on donkeys or carts. Products from the east were often brought to market on camel trains.

Wherever possible, ships were used to transport goods around the Empire. Huge ships carried the massive grain harvests of Egypt into Rome. Merchant ships like this one carried their cargoes in storage jars called *amphorae*. ▼

Each *amphora* had a pointed base so that they could be tightly packed in the ship's hold. These jars were used to carry wine, olive oil and a fish paste called *garum*.

3 The extent of the Roman Empire in AD **14**

4 The extent of the Roman Empire in AD **117**

# ROMAN SOCIETY

Rome's earliest rulers were kings. But before long, the people felt that having a king gave far too much power to one person. In 509 BC, they overthrew their last king, an Etruscan named Tarquin the Proud. The Romans decided to set up a completely new sort of government – a republic. This meant they would be ruled by officials chosen by themselves.

▲ In public, top officials were each accompanied by a *lictor*. Each lictor carried a bundle of rods and axes on his shoulder called a *fasces*. This was a symbol of the power of the official.

## ROMAN OFFICIALS

The careers of Roman officials followed a set pattern from *quaestor* through to consul. After this, they were allowed to govern part of the Empire.

**Aediles** supervised markets, public buildings and sporting events (see pages 18–19).

**SPQR**
These initials stood for the Latin words *Senatus Populusque Romanus*, which means the 'Senate and People of Rome'. The Senate was a ruling council whose members (senators) came from Rome's most important families. Two top officials, called consuls, were elected. Consuls were given power for only one year at a time to stop them becoming too powerful. There were also two councils that had some ordinary citizens as members, called the *Comitia*.

Because consuls became senators again after one year, they took care to follow the Senate's advice during their time in office.

**Tribunes of the people** looked after the interests of ordinary working people (plebeians).

**Censors** kept a register of citizens' names.

**Quaestors** dealt with state finances.

**Praetors** supervised the law courts and the provinces.

**Consuls** were the heads of state and controllers of the armies.

**Dictators** could be elected to absolute power in an emergency for six months.

## WORKERS

In the early days of Rome, most people worked for themselves as traders, farmers, craftsmen or laborers. By the end of the Republic, many of these jobs were being done by slaves. The biggest Roman industries such as mining and farming depended on them for labor. Roman towns had shops, small businesses and factories run by families with both slave and free workers. There were areas of the town with workshops devoted to one particular trade such as carpentry or metalwork. For noble people, the only respectable jobs were ones in the government or army. Most women worked in the home.

The Romans began blowing glass in the first century BC. Bottles, pots and tableware were mass-produced for everyday use.

## ROMAN LAW

Laws called the Twelve Tables were written in 451 BC about the rights and duties of citizens. People went on using Roman law for centuries after the days of the Romans.

## SLAVES

A great many people living in Rome were slaves, who had no rights. Many had been brought to Rome as prisoners of war, and others had been purchased from slave-dealers. The slaves did all the manual and unpleasant jobs. Some slaves were freed by their owners, and became citizens.

**Slave identification tag**

Slave owners were always afraid of a mass revolt like the one led by slave-gladiator Spartacus in 73 BC.

## CITIZENSHIP

One of the greatest things about being Roman was the right to be called a Roman citizen. As such, you had many privileges which were denied to non-citizens. Citizens were the only people who could vote at council meetings, and in the early days of the Republic, they were the only men who could join the army. Not all people living in Rome were citizens – many were slaves or had come to the city to trade. Eventually free men in all parts of the Empire became citizens.

The wealthiest citizens came from Rome's oldest, richest families. They were called patricians.

The middle rank of citizens were rich businessmen known as equestrians.

The poorest Roman citizens were called the plebeians. Many of them could not afford to buy even simple foods like bread and fruit. They relied on the government to provide them with free grain.

# Eminent Emperors

Julius Caesar became consul to the Roman Republic in 59 BC. He was a great general, introducing reforms to the government, and leading his armies to win Gaul (France) for Rome. Julius Caesar became dictator in 46 BC, but to many Romans this seemed like having a king again. He was stabbed to death at a meeting of the Senate in 44 BC and the era of the Republic ended.

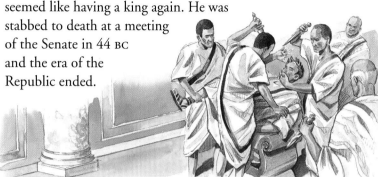

Following the murder of Julius Caesar, military leaders fought for power in Rome. Julius Caesar's nephew, Augustus, eventually took control as *princeps* or first citizen. He convinced the people that he was their equal, but gradually won power from the Senate, finally taking over in 27 BC. Augustus became the first Roman emperor. He conquered many lands for the Empire and brought peace and order to Rome.

Instead of kingly crowns, Roman emperors wore wreaths of laurel leaves. These symbolized military success and power.

## The mad and the bad

**Caligula** lived in great luxury. It was said that he drank pearls dissolved in vinegar because ordinary food wasn't good enough for him. It was even rumored that he wanted to appoint his favorite horse as consul! In the end, Caligula was murdered by his soldiers.

**Tiberius** terrified his people. He employed spies to inform on his subjects; even a few careless words about the emperor could result in torture or a death sentence.

**Nero** is believed to have set fire to Rome in AD 64. He blamed the Christians, and many were put to death.

## Triumphant emperors

After a great battle, an emperor was given a triumph – a victory parade through Rome. He wore special clothes: a purple tunic embroidered with gold and a crown of laurel leaves. A slave held a golden crown from the statue of Jupiter over his head.

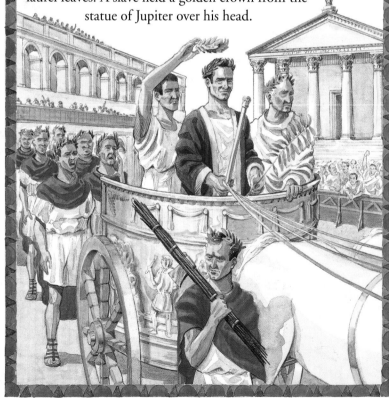

## MIGHT AND MONUMENTS

Emperors often built statues, temples and arches to remind people how powerful they were. They initiated building projects such as Vespasian's Colosseum, or Trajan's famous column. Even the pictures on coins were used to tell people that the emperor was a man to be feared.

**Claudius** was ignored because he limped and stuttered. However, the army proclaimed him emperor after Caligula's murder. He restored order in Rome and his armies conquered many new lands. ▶

◀ **Vespasian** restored order to Rome after the civil wars following Nero's death. He ordered a program of public buildings in Rome, including the Colosseum.

**Trajan** was a soldier-emperor who was famous for winning battles. His victories were recorded in stone carvings on a great column in Rome. ▶

◀ **Hadrian** visited thirty-eight Roman provinces, making sure the frontiers of his Empire were well-protected.

**Diocletian** divided the Empire into two. He ruled the Eastern Empire from Constantinople, and appointed another ruler in Rome to control the west. ▶

◀ **Constantine** was the first emperor to be converted to Christianity. In AD 330 he moved his capital from Rome to Constantinople.

## WHO WAS EMPEROR?

**50 BC**

**Julius Caesar** establishes the first Triumvirate (rule by three people) 59 BC – murdered 44 BC; Republic ends
**Augustus** rules 27 BC – AD 14, as first emperor

**0**

**Tiberius** AD 14–37
**Caligula** AD 37–41
**Claudius** AD 41–54
**AD 50** **Nero** AD 54–68
**Vespasian** AD 69–79
**Titus** AD 79–81
**Domitian** AD 81–96
**Nerva** AD 96–98

**AD 100** **Trajan** AD 98–117
**Hadrian** AD 117–138

**Antoninus Pius** AD 138–161

**AD 150**

**Marcus Aurelius** AD 161–180

**Commodus** AD 180–192
**Septimius Severus** AD 193–211
**AD 200**
**Caracalla** AD 212–217
**Elagabalus** AD 218–222
**Severus Alexander** AD 222–235
Nearly twenty emperors rule during the
**AD 250** years AD 235–284

**AD 250**

**Diocletian** AD 284–306

**AD 300** **Constantine the Great** AD 306–337

**AD 350**

**Julian the Apostate** AD 360–363

**Theodosius the Great** AD 378–395

**AD 400**

15

# ROMAN LIFE

Wealthy Romans lived in spacious, comfortable houses with underfloor heating to keep them warm in winter. They often had magnificent villas on country estates or by the sea. In towns and cities, people lived in rented apartments or flats, in blocks up to six stories high. Poorer families had only one or two rooms to live in.

A villa on an estate in the countryside

## ROMAN FAMILIES

Roman law gave men complete authority over all the members of the family. Boys were considered to be of more use than a girl; wealthy boys attended school from the age of seven to about eleven. Some went on to learn the family business. Most girls were taught how to run a household by their mothers.

## LIFE IN THE CITY

Towns and cities were busy places. Streets were lined with shops and taverns selling hot food and wine. Only the rich had water piped to their houses; everyone else used water from public fountains. They also used the public lavatories, which were built around the town and connected to underground sewers.

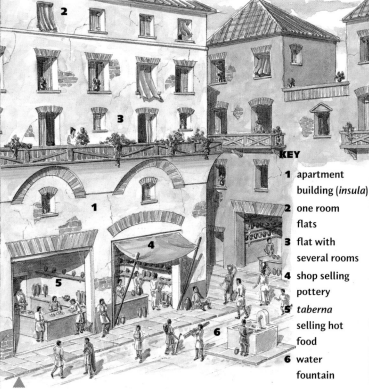

**KEY**

1 apartment building (*insula*)
2 one room flats
3 flat with several rooms
4 shop selling pottery
5 *taberna* selling hot food
6 water fountain

Most town dwellers lived in large apartment buildings, or *insulae*, anything up to seven stories high.

Wealthy people lived on the ground floors of insulae. This plan shows a typical layout. ▼

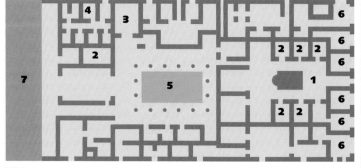

**KEY**

1 hall (*atrium*)
2 bedrooms
3 dining room (*triclinium*)
4 slaves' room
5 courtyard with pool (*peristyle*)
6 shops on street
7 covered porch (*portico*)

## GOOD FOOD

Wealthy Romans enjoyed good food. These menus show a typical daily diet for a rich Roman family.

**Breakfast**
bread and fruit

**Lunch**
cheese, cold fish or meat, and vegetables

**Dinner**
seafood, snails or eggs to start; roast meat for the main course; sweets and fruit for dessert

Poorer families ate simpler meals, of bread, porridge, olives, onions, garlic, cheese, salt fish and fruit. Most of them could not afford meat. People could not cook in their homes because of the risk of fire, so if they wanted hot food they bought it from 'take-outs'.

## BANQUETS

Rich Romans liked to invite friends to banquets. Guests reclined on couches around low tables, and were waited on by slaves. There were seven courses and different wines. People ate with their fingers or with spoons. Appetizers included salads, eggs and jellyfish. Main courses were meat, perhaps venison, stuffed flamingos, parrots or dormice. For dessert there were cakes, fruits and nuts. Some guests went outside to make themselves sick so that they could eat more food!

## ROMAN DRESS

All Romans wore leather sandals, shoes and boots.

Roman citizens wore a robe called a toga. It was normally white and made of a piece of wool or linen. Colors were used for special occasions or to show people's rank.

Women wore jewelry made from gold and precious and semi-precious stones. They also used make-up made from vegetable and mineral dyes. Chalk was used as a face powder.

During the Empire, men and women had elaborately curled hairstyles. Women often wore wigs made from the hair of foreign slaves.

 Bracelet shaped like a snake

Brooch (*fibula*) to fasten a cloak or a tunic

Women wore a dress called a *stola* over the top of a tunic. Sometimes they wore a shawl, or *palla* on top.

Togas were semi-circular in shape and were draped over the body.

A senator's toga had a purple stripe.

A rich boy's toga had a purple border.

The emperor's toga was purple with gold embroidery.

A brightly colored toga for a special occasion.

A dark toga for mourning the dead.

A simple tunic was always worn under a toga.

# ROMANS AT PLAY

A quarter of the days in the Roman year were holidays. People enjoyed watching fights between gladiators at the amphitheaters, chariot races at the circus, and going to the theater and to the baths. Many of the shows were paid for by wealthy citizens or the government. With up to 150,000 poor and unemployed people in Rome, free entertainment was intended to prevent rioting.

## GLADIATORS

Gladiator fights were among the most popular entertainments. They were held in amphitheaters such as the Colosseum (see pages 7 and 25). The ground was covered in sand so that the blood could be cleared away. There were many different types of gladiators.

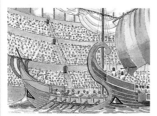

Sometimes, amphitheaters were flooded and spectacular naval battles were reconstructed.

**A Samnite** carrying a sword and shield

**A Thracian** with a dagger and small, round shield

**A murmillo**, heavily armed and much feared

**A retiarius** carrying a net and trident to fight with

## CHARIOT RACING

In Rome, chariot races were held in a huge stadium, the Circus Maximus, which held 250,000 people. Chariots were drawn by teams of horses and driven by a charioteer. The signal to start the race was given by a consul or other top official, who threw a white cloth from his seat onto the track. The chariots raced round the *spina*, the 'backbone' down the middle of the Circus. The turn at each end of the track was very tight and accidents were common. Competition was fierce, with betting on the winners. A day at the races included acrobatic displays, music, and other entertainments.

### KEY

1 *spina*

2 charioteers racing seven laps of the course

3 the emperor and his family sitting in the Imperial box

4 crowds cheering on their chosen team

5 a chariot accident

People watched fights between men and animals, or just between animals, in amphitheaters. Wild animals were brought to Rome from Africa and the East: bears, buffalos, elephants, leopards, tigers and rhinos. So many were needed that it was difficult to keep up with the demand.

# GAMES

Romans loved playing sports as well as watching them. Men practiced running, jumping, wrestling and throwing and played ball games. In the countryside, people fished and the wealthy hunted deer and wild boar. Children played with toy animals, dolls, marbles and hoops.

Knucklebones was played by throwing and scoring from numbered pieces of glass, pottery or bronze.

## THE BATHS

Public baths were built in all the main cities. Men and women enjoyed going to the baths, not just to get clean, but to meet friends and gossip, or play games. Mixed bathing was not allowed: men and women bathed at separate times. First, people bathed in a steaming pool of hot water (*caldarium*), then relaxed in a warm pool (*tepidarium*), then a cold pool (*frigidarium*).

Relaxing by the poolside at the *frigidarium* after a cold swim ▶

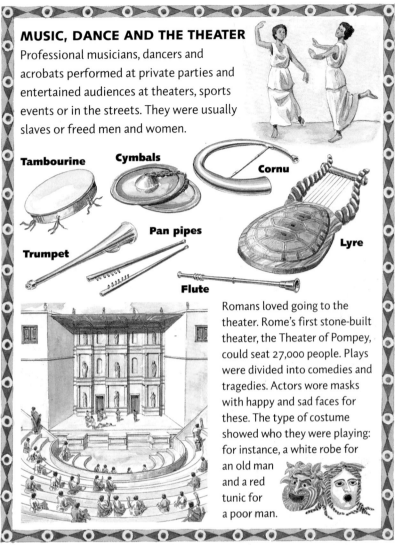

## MUSIC, DANCE AND THE THEATER

Professional musicians, dancers and acrobats performed at private parties and entertained audiences at theaters, sports events or in the streets. They were usually slaves or freed men and women.

**Tambourine**  **Cymbals**  **Cornu**
**Trumpet**  **Pan pipes**  **Lyre**  **Flute**

Romans loved going to the theater. Rome's first stone-built theater, the Theater of Pompey, could seat 27,000 people. Plays were divided into comedies and tragedies. Actors wore masks with happy and sad faces for these. The type of costume showed who they were playing: for instance, a white robe for an old man and a red tunic for a poor man.

# GODS AND GODDESSES

The Romans believed in lots of different gods and goddesses. Each was supposed to look after a different aspect of their lives. The gods were not expected to be kind. They could be bad-tempered and selfish, just like ordinary humans. People feared the gods; they believed they could easily be angered, and then all sorts of misfortunes could happen. The Romans worshiped their gods and made sacrifices to them in special ceremonies carried out by priests, who were chosen from high-ranking families.

## LARES AND PENATES

Lares and Penates were gods in charge of each household. Many houses had a little shrine in honor of them, and food was put out as offerings to them.

## GODS AND SPIRITS

The Romans believed that the spirits of dead ancestors had to be fed and looked after. To add to the other gods they worshiped, they adopted foreign gods from the Greeks, Egyptians and Persians. When they started to believe in the Christian God, they gradually gave up belief in their old gods.

**Juno**, goddess of women and childbirth

**Mars**, god of war

**Minerva**, goddess of wisdom and war

**Venus**, goddess of love, beauty and fertility

**Jupiter**, god of skies, rain, thunder and patron god of Rome

**Mercury**, messenger of the gods and god of business

**Apollo**, god of the sun and patron of music and poetry

**Bacchus**, god of fertility and of wine

**Ceres**, goddess of growth and crops

**Diana**, goddess of the moon and hunting

**Isis**, Egyptian goddess of eternal life

Worshipers came to watch and take part. They brought gifts of food.

Animals were decorated with garlands ready to be sacrificed.

## GETTING IN TOUCH WITH THE GODS

The Romans were very superstitious. They believed that some days were unlucky, and that any activity carried out on those days would be sure to fail. They worked out ways to communicate with the gods. One way was to use people known as *horuspices* to inspect the livers of dead animals – this was called 'divination'. Another way was for *augurs* to study the flight and calls of birds – this was called 'taking the auspices'.

## FEASTS AND FESTIVALS

The Romans set many public holidays aside to celebrate festivals of gods and goddesses. Animals were sacrificed at altars outside temples, and processions and great feasts were held. ▼

## TEMPLES

Temples stood on a high platform, with steps leading from an altar up to the front. At the front, there was a covered area with columns holding up the roof. Behind this was a large room containing a statue of the god or gods to whom the temple was dedicated.

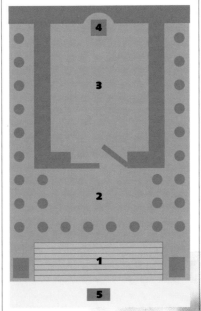

**KEY**

**1** steps
**2** covered area with columns
**3** large room
**4** statue
**5** altar

## THE TEMPLE OF VESTA

The temple of the goddess Vesta was one of the most important buildings in Rome. A fire was always kept burning here. Vesta was served by priestesses from noble families, called Vestals. It was a great honor to be a Vestal. But if these priestesses disgraced the goddess, they could be buried alive as punishment.

Musicians played until the moment of the sacrifice.

The animals were killed with a sacred knife.

Priests watched to check that everything was done correctly.

Altars stood in front of temples. The smoke from burning incense and holy oil was meant to carry the offering up to the gods.

# ROMANS AT WAR

The great strength of the Roman army was its organized legions of foot soldiers. Each legion consisted of groups of about 5,000 footsoldiers called legionaries. Only Roman citizens could apply to be legionaries. After a demanding and often brutal training period, they were ready to fight for their emperor and Empire.

## WHO WAS IN CHARGE?

The legion commander was known as a legate.

Then came six officers called tribunes. The senior tribune commanded the legion in the legate's absence.

Next in command was the prefect of the camp, who looked after equipment and engineering works, such as building camps.

Each legion had its own standard bearer and trumpeter.

Each century (page 23) was commanded by a centurion

## A ROMAN LEGIONARY - THE BACKBONE OF THE EMPIRE

A legionary had to carry enough equipment and food to survive for up to three days in hostile lands. He carried his supplies on a pole over his shoulder. Besides armor, weapons and food, each legionary carried tools for building roads and defenses.

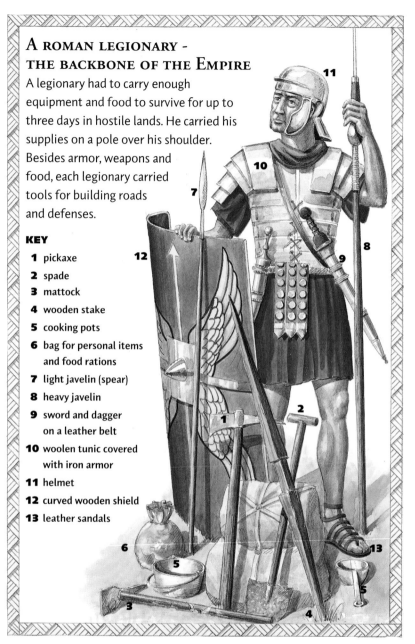

### KEY

**1** pickaxe
**2** spade
**3** mattock
**4** wooden stake
**5** cooking pots
**6** bag for personal items and food rations
**7** light javelin (spear)
**8** heavy javelin
**9** sword and dagger on a leather belt
**10** woolen tunic covered with iron armor
**11** helmet
**12** curved wooden shield
**13** leather sandals

## TRAINING

Each new army recruit was first taught to march and build a camp. He would be expected to march for 20 miles, three times a month. Legionaries were also given training in stone-slinging, swimming and horse-riding. They were then expected to serve in the army for twenty-five years.

## ARMY ORGANIZATION

A legion was a highly organized fighting team. Legions were backed up by auxiliary troops who served as border guards, archers and horsemen.

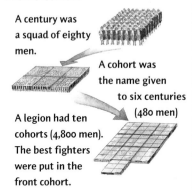

A century was a squad of eighty men.

A cohort was the name given to six centuries (480 men)

A legion had ten cohorts (4,800 men). The best fighters were put in the front cohort.

## READY FOR BATTLE

Legionaries fought on foot with two long javelins (spears) and a short stabbing sword. They were divided into three battle lines; the front line threw their spears first. Then the best troops, who were positioned in the second line, threw their swords. They tried to smash their way through the center of the enemy line. Out of sight of the enemy, the third line knelt down. They thrust their spears forward, ready to fight if the second line needed help.

▲ The Romans often used a 'tortoise' formation so that they could march safely towards the enemy.

▲ A *ballista* was a catapult which hurled arrows with iron tips at the enemy. The arrows were so large and heavy that they pierced the strongest armor and could travel a long way.

## ATTACK!

The Romans had two methods of capturing towns – by blockade or by assault. They constructed blockades of towers and fences around towns and attacked until the enemy surrendered. Here, the army is assaulting a town using a battering ram to break down enemy walls (**1**) and a large catapult (*onager*) to hurl big rocks (**2**). Scaling ladders (**3**) and siege-towers (**4**) are being used to climb over the walls. Galleys (**5**) are protecting soldiers as they move forward.

## SLEEPING SAFELY

The Romans built forts as they traveled, to protect their troops as they ate, slept and rested. Early forts were built of wood. Soldiers dug ditches, made ramparts and put up fences at the end of a days' march. Later forts were built in stone. As each fort was built to a similar design, soldiers could find their way around easily, wherever they were stationed.

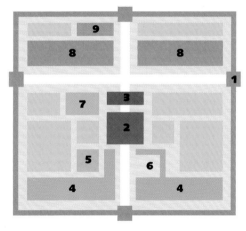

**KEY**

**1** gates and walls
**2** commander's house (*praetorium*)
**3** offices (*principia*)
**4** barracks
**5** workshops
**6** market place
**7** hospital
**8** tribunes' houses
**9** granary and kitchen

# Buildings, Engineering and Inventions

The Romans were skilled builders and engineers. They planned and laid out new cities, providing public lavatories and baths, good drains and a constant supply of water for the townspeople. Many of their constructions are still standing today.

Slaves cut out stone blocks from quarries by drilling holes and filling them with wooden wedges. Water swelled the wood and split the stone.

## Making arches

To build an arch, a curved wooden support was put at the top of two stone columns.

Wedge-shaped stones were put around the support. When it was taken away, the arch stayed up on its own.

## Roads

Engineers built 50,000 miles of roads, to link all parts of the Empire to Rome. The roads enabled soldiers to move about the Empire, but they were also used by merchants. Roman roads took the shortest, straightest routes possible. Some roads involved tunneling through hills and cutting across valleys.

## AQUEDUCTS AND BRIDGES

The Romans were very skilled at building aqueducts and bridges. Aqueducts brought water to cities from springs and lakes in the hills. The Romans realized that they could use gravity to bring the water down to towns at lower levels. Eleven aqueducts brought water to Rome, from up to 30 miles away. Over 900 million gallons of water were brought to the city every day to supply fountains, baths and private houses.

Aqueduct at Segovia

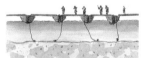

**1** To make a river crossing, first a temporary bridge was laid across a row of boats.

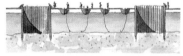

**2** Then circles of wooden stakes were sunk into the river bed and the water pumped out of the space inside.

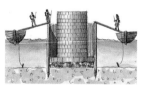

**3** These spaces were filled with columns of stone blocks.

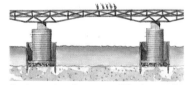

**4** A wooden frame was lifted onto the columns by cranes to form the bridge.

**1** First, surveyors used a *groma* to make sure the land was level and marked out the road with stakes.

**2** Then a trench, up to 40 feet wide, was dug and workmen laid curbstones along the edges.

**3** The trench was packed with sand, then stones, then rubble. These layers formed the foundation of the road.

**4** The top layer of stone slabs, added to make the road's surface, was curved to allow rain to drain off.

## BIGGEST BUILDINGS

**The Colosseum**, in Rome, was an enormous amphitheater built to stage gladiator fights. It seated crowds of up to 50,000 people and took ten years to build.

**The Pantheon** was a temple with a large, circular hall. It was one of the most famous buildings of ancient times because of its vast domed roof, 141 feet in diameter. Built between AD 118 and 128, it has been used as a place of worship ever since.

**The Baths of Caracalla**, in Rome were built on a grand scale. The main hall was enormous, over 100 x 25 yards in size. The baths could take up to 1,600 bathers every day. The buildings included shops, offices, libraries, gymnasiums and sports facilities.

**Hadrian's Wall**, a fortified wall 75 miles long, was built across northern Britain to keep out warring tribes. The wall was of stone, up to 10 feet thick, with fortified positions along its length.

## CENTRAL HEATING

Wealthy Romans enjoyed central heating thanks to underfloor heating systems called hypocausts. Floors were supported on piles of bricks, with space underneath for air to circulate. A fire sent hot air into this space, warming the rooms above. Hypocausts were used in public baths as well as private houses. ▼

## WHEN WERE THEY BUILT?

**First road and first aqueduct constructed in Rome** 312 BC

100 BC

50 BC — **First stone theater built in Rome** 55 BC

**Julius Caesar builds a new forum in Rome** 46 BC

**Pont du Gard aqueduct built in Nîmes, Gaul** 20–16 BC

**Theater of Marcellus built in Rome** 13–11 BC

0

AD 50

**Fire destroys many of Rome's buildings** AD 64

**Work on the Colosseum in Rome finishes** AD 79

**Trajan's Column built in Rome** AD 98

AD 100 — **Aqueduct at Segovia constructed in Spain** AD 100

**Hadrian builds a great villa at Tivoli near Rome** AD 118

**Pantheon in Rome built** AD 118–128

**Hadrian's Wall in Britain built** AD 122–138

AD 150

**Trajan's Column**

AD 200 — **Baths of Caracalla in Rome built** AD 212–216

AD 250

# WORDS AND PICTURES

Latin was the language of the Romans. It was used in the army and for government business throughout the Empire. The conquered peoples of the Empire were eager to learn it, and because of its widespread use, Latin became a common language in many parts of the ancient world. After the fall of Rome and the spread of the Christian Church, Latin continued to be the international language of western Europe. It is still used, especially in science and the law.

The Romans admired men who could speak well in public. This skill was called oratory. Learning oratory was part of a Roman's education.

## ROMANI VNICO ASPECTV

▲ This script says 'Ancient Romans at a glance' in Latin.

## ROMAN WRITING

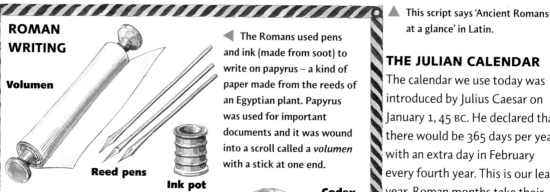

**Volumen**

**Reed pens**

**Ink pot**

**Codex**

◀ The Romans used pens and ink (made from soot) to write on papyrus – a kind of paper made from the reeds of an Egyptian plant. Papyrus was used for important documents and it was wound into a scroll called a *volumen* with a stick at one end.

Later, sheets of thin animal skin called vellum and parchment were used to make bound books. ▶

Romans sometimes wrote on paper-thin pieces of wood. Soldiers often used these pieces of wood to write home. ▶

**Wax tablet**

**Stylus**

◀ Another method the Romans used was to write on a small wooden tablet covered with a layer of beeswax. They scratched their message on it, using a pointed tool called a *stylus*. After the message had been read, the beeswax could be smoothed over and used again. Children used these wax tablets in schools.

## THE JULIAN CALENDAR

The calendar we use today was introduced by Julius Caesar on January 1, 45 BC. He declared that there would be 365 days per year with an extra day in February every fourth year. This is our leap year. Roman months take their names from eminent Romans, gods and numbers. ▼

| January | **Januarius** |
| February | **Februarius** |
| March | **Martius** |
| April | **Aprilis** |
| May | **Maius** |
| June | **Junius** |
| July | **Julius** (named after Julius Caesar) |
| August | **Augustus** (named after the Emperor Augustus) |
| September | **September** |
| October | **October** |
| November | **November** |
| December | **December** |

## ART AND ARTISTS

The Romans enjoyed art, as we know from the many statues and wall-paintings that can still be seen. Wealthy Romans paid sculptors and painters to decorate their homes and gardens.

◀ Sculptors worked in bronze and stone, producing life-like statues of emperors, famous people, or gods and goddesses.

Artists painted landscapes and scenes from nature, often covering entire walls or ceilings in the houses of wealthy people. To do this they used a technique called *fresco*, which involved painting onto wet plaster before it had quite dried. This meant they had to work very quickly. ▼

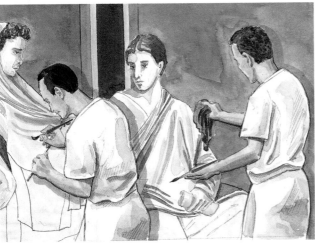

Other artists covered floors and walls with beautiful mosaic pictures. These were made from thousands of small colored cubes of stone, brick or glass called *tesserae*. ▶

### ROMAN NUMBERS

| | | | | | | | |
|---|---|---|---|---|---|---|---|
| I | 1 | V | 5 | IX | 9 | L | 50 |
| II | 2 | VI | 6 | X | 10 | C | 100 |
| III | 3 | VII | 7 | XI | 11 | D | 500 |
| IV | 4 | VIII | 8 | XII | 12 | M | 1000 |

## WHO WROTE IN ROME?

**100 BC**

**Cicero** (106–43 BC) – a famous orator and writer on politics and philosophy

**Julius Caesar** (100–44 BC) – a general who wrote an account of his wars in Gaul

**Virgil** (70–19 BC) – a poet who wrote the *Aeneid*, the story of the founding of Rome

**Horace** (65–8 BC) – a great poet and satirist whose work includes the *Odes*

**50 BC**

**Cicero**

**0**

**Seneca the Younger** (4 BC–AD 65) – a philosopher, statesman and playwright

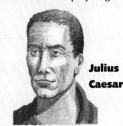

**Julius Caesar**

**AD 50**

**Tacitus** (AD 55–120) – one of the greatest historians who ever lived; he wrote a history of the Roman Empire from AD 69–96

**Pliny the Younger** (AD 62–113) – an orator and writer; he wrote many letters from which we have learned a great deal about Rome

**AD 100**

**Pliny the Younger**

# THE END OF THE EMPIRE

By the end of the fourth century, Rome had been under attack from outsiders for a long time. Roman power in the west began to crumble, as barbarians moved into Roman lands. The barbarians had been pushed out of their homelands by the Huns, a warrior people from the east. Now they were looking for new areas where they could settle. In AD 406 the Vandals and other tribes crossed the River Rhine, pushing towards France and Spain. The Goths invaded Rome in AD 410 and devastated the city. Soon these peoples were setting up their own kingdoms in what had been Roman lands.

## POWER STRUGGLES

When Rome was at its most powerful, the emperor was always obeyed. But from the end of the fourth century, this changed. The emperor could not stop the barbarians from taking Roman land – as the Vandals did in Africa and the Visigoths in Gaul. Rival emperors began to fight each other for power.

## THE FIRST CHRISTIAN EMPEROR

From AD 305 the Empire was torn apart by civil wars. After beating a rival emperor in battle, Constantine (c. AD 274–337) became a Christian. He ordered that Christians throughout the Empire should be left in peace to follow their religion. In AD 324 he declared Christianity the state religion. Constantine founded the new capital city in the east, Constantinople.

## THE SPREAD OF CHRISTIANITY

Christianity was different from other religions at that time. It was based on the teachings of a real person, Jesus of Nazareth, and the events surrounding his life. The Romans believed that Jesus and his teachings threatened their rule in Palestine and they executed him by crucifixion in Jerusalem in about AD 33. Christianity spread rapidly throughout the Empire, although at first the emperors opposed it and ordered Christian worship to be banned.

Crucifixion was a common form of execution during the days of the Empire. It was normally slaves and people with no rights who were crucified. They were flogged, then nailed to a wooden cross. It could take two to three days for them to die. The cross became the symbol of the Christian faith.

Barbarians set up new kingdoms in Roman lands.

## THE EMPIRE IN THE EAST

When Roman power was finally lost in the west, there was still an Empire in the east. It was called the Byzantine Empire and was ruled from Constantinople (modern-day Istanbul in Turkey). The Eastern Empire remained until 1453, but it was different to the Empire ruled from Rome; the language spoken was Greek and the main religion was Christianity.

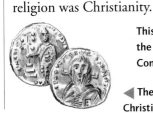

This gold statuette represented the capital of the Eastern Empire, Constantinople. ▲

◄ These gold coins bear the Christian images of the new Empire.

## THE LAST YEARS OF THE EMPIRE AT A GLANCE

**AD 330**  City of Constantinople founded

**AD 395**  The Empire permanently divided into two parts, east and west

**AD 406–7**  Sueves and Vandals invade Spain

**AD 409**  Alans and Vandals invade Spain

**AD 410**  Rome itself attacked by Alaric the Goth

**AD 419**  Visigoths set up their own kingdom in Spain

**AD 429**  Vandals set up their own kingdom in Africa

**AD 452**  Attila the Hun and his men invade Italy

**AD 455**  Vandals sack Rome

**AD 476**  Last emperor of Rome, Romulus Augustulus, overthrown

## ROME'S ENEMIES

**1 The Huns** were the most feared warriors throughout Europe during the fourth century. They were skilled archers and horseriders. They defeated many German tribes and fought for the Romans until their leader, Attila, launched an attack on the Empire in AD 441. The Huns had not been paid by the Romans and Attila ordered the sacking of many Italian cities.

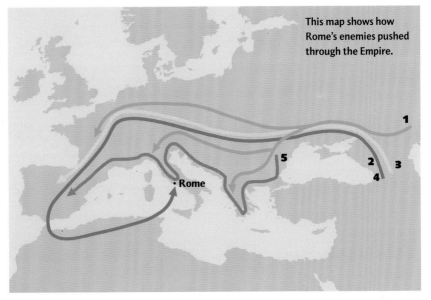

This map shows how Rome's enemies pushed through the Empire.

Rome

**2 The Vandals** set up kingdoms around the Roman Empire in Spain, Gaul and North Africa after fleeing from the Huns in their homeland, Germany. They sacked Rome in AD 455.

**3 The Sueves** were a German people who settled in Roman Spain between AD 409–447. They were chased from their homelands by the Huns.

**4 The Alans** were frequent raiders of Parthia in the fourth century. When they were defeated by the Huns, they settled in North Africa with the Vandals.

**5 The Visigoths** raided the Roman Empire for centuries. They established great kingdoms in Gaul and Spain and invaded Italy repeatedly from AD 401, sacking Rome in AD 410.

# GLOSSARY

**Amphitheater** A circular building with rows of seats surrounding a central space

**Aqueduct** A raised channel for carrying water

**Augurs** Religious officials in Rome who interpreted the wishes of the gods by studying the behavior of birds

**Barbarian** Describing members of wild, uncivilized tribes

**Circus** In Roman times, a large circular building with rows of seats around an arena where chariot races and contests took place

**Consuls** The chief officials of the Senate

**Dictator** An all-powerful ruler

**Gladiators** In Ancient Rome, men trained to fight each other with various weapons, to entertain the people

**Hypocaust** A form of under-floor heating in Roman times

**Javelin** A light throwing spear

**Legions** Groups of 3,000 to 6,000 foot soldiers in the Roman army

**Magistrates** People who have the power to enforce laws

**Mosaics** Pictures made by sticking small pieces of colored stone or glass on to floors and walls

**Orators** Public speakers

**Pagan** In the ancient world, anyone who was not a Christian

**Provinces** Territories outside Italy ruled by a Roman governor

**Ramparts** Defensive walls

**Republic** A form of government where the people choose their own rulers

**Senate** The special council which ruled Rome

**Soothsayers** People who could predict future happenings

**Toga** A loose, flowing garment worn by citizens of Ancient Rome

**Viaduct** A series of stone arches, carrying a road across a valley

# INDEX

## A
Alexandria 8, 9
amphitheaters 18
*amphorae* 11
animals 11, 18, 19, 21
aqueducts 7, 8, 9, 24
arches 24
army 22–23
art 27
Athens 8, 9
Augustus 7, 10, 14

## B
*ballista* 23
banquets 17
barbarians 9, 28, 29
baths 19, 25
battles 18, 23
bridges 24
buildings 16, 19, 25

## C
calendar 26
Caligula 14
camel trains 11
Caracalla, Baths of 9, 25
Carthage 7, 8, 9
central heating 25
chariot racing 18
children 19, 26
Christianity 15, 28
Cicero 27
Circus Maximus 9, 18
citizenship 13
city life 16
Claudius 15
clothes 17
coins 11, 29
Colosseum 7, 9, 15, 25
Constantine 7, 9, 15, 28
Constantinople 7, 8, 9, 28, 29
consuls 12
cooking 17

## D
dancers 19
dictators 12, 14
Diocletian 15

## E
Emperors 9,10,11,14–15, 17, 18, 28
enemies 28, 29
engineering 24
entertainment 18–19
equestrians 13

## F
family life 16
fashion 17
feasts 17, 21
festivals 21
food 13, 17, 20
forts 23
*frescos* 27

## G
games 19
gladiators 7, 18
gods 20–21
government 12

## H
Hadrian 15
Hadrian's Wall 7, 9, 25
hairstyles 17
Herculaneum 7, 8, 9
Horace 27
houses 16, 20

## I
*insulae* 16
inventions 24, 25

## J
Jerusalem 9
jewelry 17
Julius Caesar 13, 14, 26, 27

## L
Lares 20
Latin 26
law 13, 16
*lictor* 12

## M
make-up 17
monuments 15
mosaics 27
music 19

## N
Nero 14, 15
Nîmes 8, 9
numbers 27

## O
officials 12
oratory 26
Ostia 8, 9, 10

## P
Pantheon 25
Parthia 9
patricians 13
Penates 20
plebeians 13
Pliny 27
Pompeii 7, 8, 9
postal service 10
priests 20, 21

## R
Ravenna 8, 9
religion 20–21
roads 24, 25
Roman Empire 8–9, 10–11, 28–29
Rome 7, 8, 9, 10, 12, 13, 14, 15, 18, 21, 24, 25, 28
Romulus and Remus 6, 9

## S
sacrifices 21
sculptures 27
Segovia 8, 9
Senate, the 12, 14
Seneca 27
ships 11
slaves 13, 16, 19
social classes 13
soldiers 22, 23
stone 24
superstition 21

## T
Tacitus 27
temples 21, 25
theater 19
Tiberius 14
togas 17
trade 10
training 22
Trajan 15
transport 11
Trier 8, 9
triumph parade 14

## V
Vespasian 15
Vesta 21
Vesuvius 7, 9
villas 16
Virgil 27

## W
war 22–23
wax tablets 26
weapons 22, 23
women 16, 17